How to use this book

The drawings in this book have been made for you to trace, carbon, reverse, copy and enlarge. They are not intended for cutting out or to be displayed from the book.

Most of the drawings are simple enough to make tracing, copying and enlarging easy.

The figures in the section on ACTION POSES (Book 1) wear a plain robe so that their body position can be seen clearly. When you have studied the sections on CLOTHES (Book 1) and CHARACTERS (Book 2), you can dress your selected action figures in the appropriate attire, or alter the costumed figure to the pose required.

The INDEX will help you to choose the figures you need. Basic characters and age studies have been drawn so you will find that one figure will serve for several characters.

Always colour your visual aids. For backgrounds, see the hints given under the heading EASY BACKGROUNDS. For figures, the best results are painted on with coloured drawing inks. Coloured pencils and fibre tip pens are quicker and easier to use but do not give such neat or striking results. Use orange paint or ink watered-down, if you cannot get a flesh coloured crayon or pen.

Identification of story characters by colour is an effective method when using simple or silhouette figures. Use a light colour (yellow, cream or white) for Jesus's robe, and darker colours for other characters. Keep reds and purples for royalty, soldiers and officials or the key characters in your story. Women generally wore a blue dress and white headdress. Plain robes can be varied by drawing on coloured borders or braids, or by making the material striped.

Make use of the backgrounds shown. Most of them have suggested figures to use with them. By tracing several figures onto them you can build up a good frieze or picture. Use the notes and suggestions on the following pages, and try to be inventive. By moving your tracing paper about, part of one figure can be used with part of another. Rearrange faces, arms and legs to suit what you need.

FALCON

Contents

Book 1

HOW TO USE THIS BOOK
**KNOW-HOW PAGES
ARRANGEMENT OF
ILLUSTRATIONS
INDEX (ALPHABETICAL)
ACTION POSES: 1–80
CLOTHES: 81–110**

Book 2

HOW TO USE THIS BOOK
**CHARACTERS: 111–197
TRADES AND
RECREATIONS: 198–246
OCCUPATIONS: 247–290
TRANSPORT: 291–301**

Book 3

HOW TO USE THIS BOOK
**PLANTS AND CREATURES:
302–404
BUILDINGS AND
BACKGROUNDS: 405–440
LIST OF ILLUSTRATIONS
(NUMERICAL)**

HOW TO USE THIS BOOK/CONTENTS

Characters

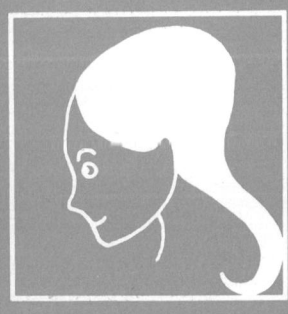

Faces, expressions:
111–134

Young men, maidens:
135–142

Children, old men:
143–154

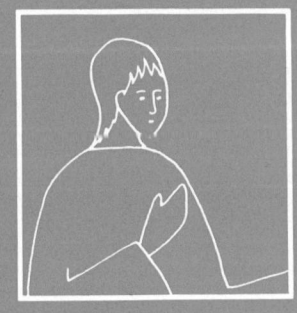

Angels, messengers:
155–158

Kings, queens:
159–166

Romans, Egyptians:
167–182

Soldiers:
183–189

Slaves, masters:
190–197

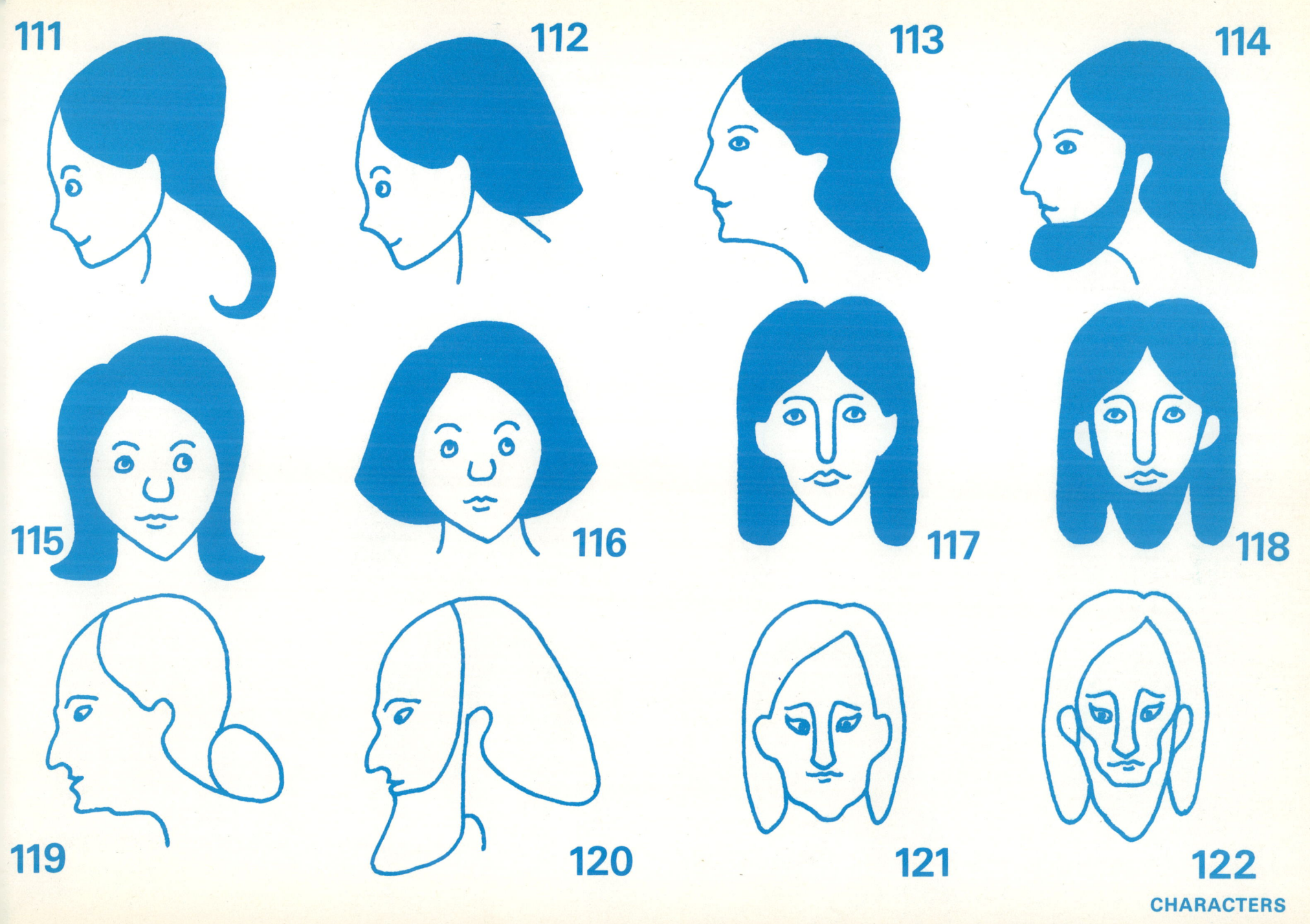

111 112 113 114

115 116 117 118

119 120 121 122

CHARACTERS

123

124

125

126

127

128

129

130

131

132

133

134

CHARACTERS

135   136   137   138

CHARACTERS

139   140   141   142

CHARACTERS

145

147

144

146

143

CHARACTERS

148   149   150

CHARACTERS

151 *Abraham*

152 *Aaron*

153

154

CHARACTERS

155

156

157

158

Artaxerxes.

159   160   161   162

163

164

165

166

CHARACTERS

167 168 169 170

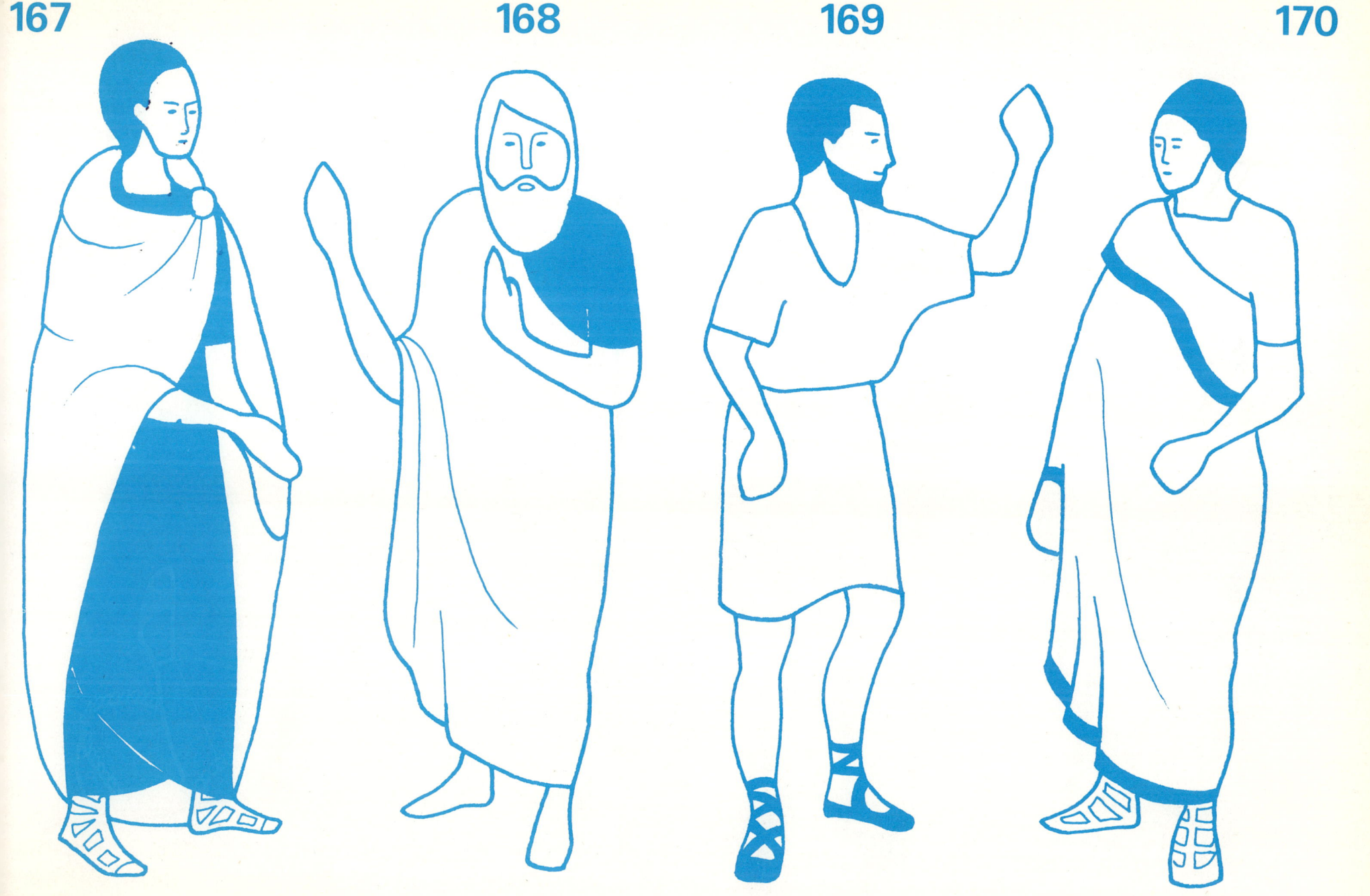

CHARACTERS

171   172   173   174

CHARACTERS

175 176 177 178

CHARACTERS

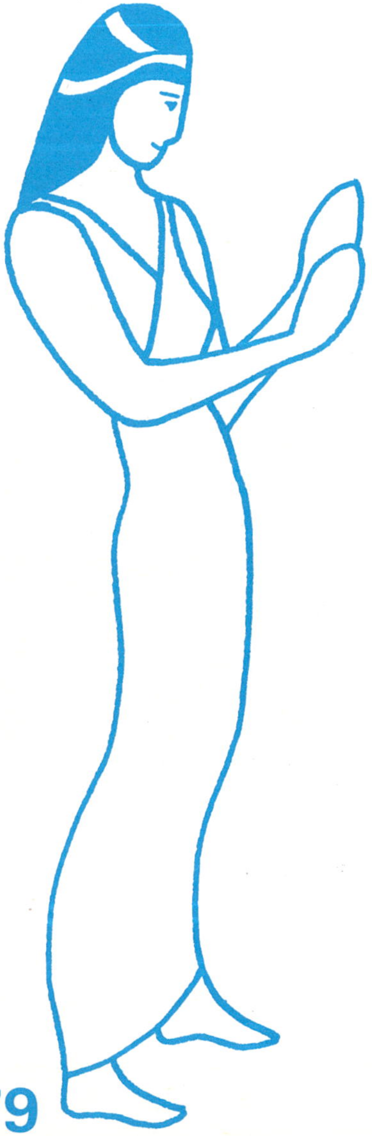

181

182

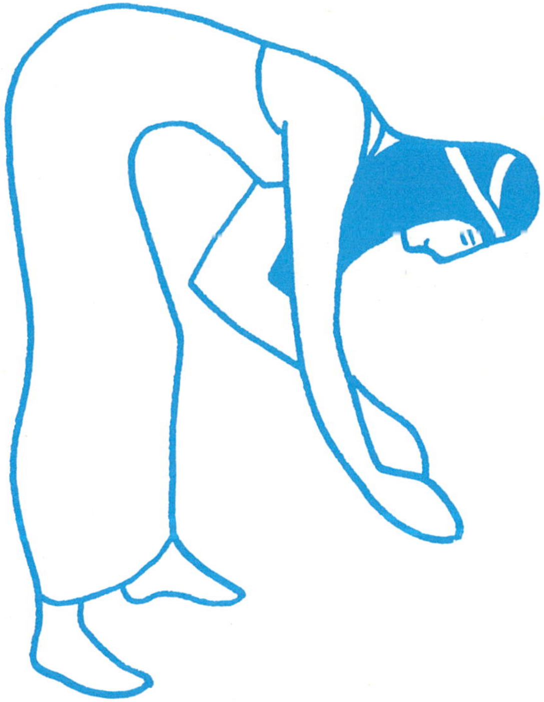

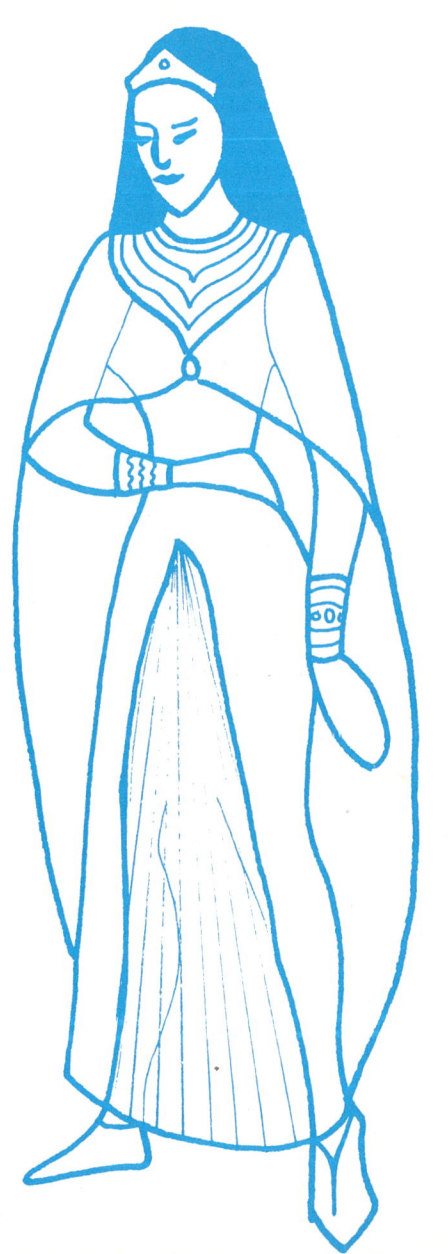

179

180

CHARACTERS

183   184   185

CHARACTERS

186   187   188

CHARACTERS

CHARACTERS

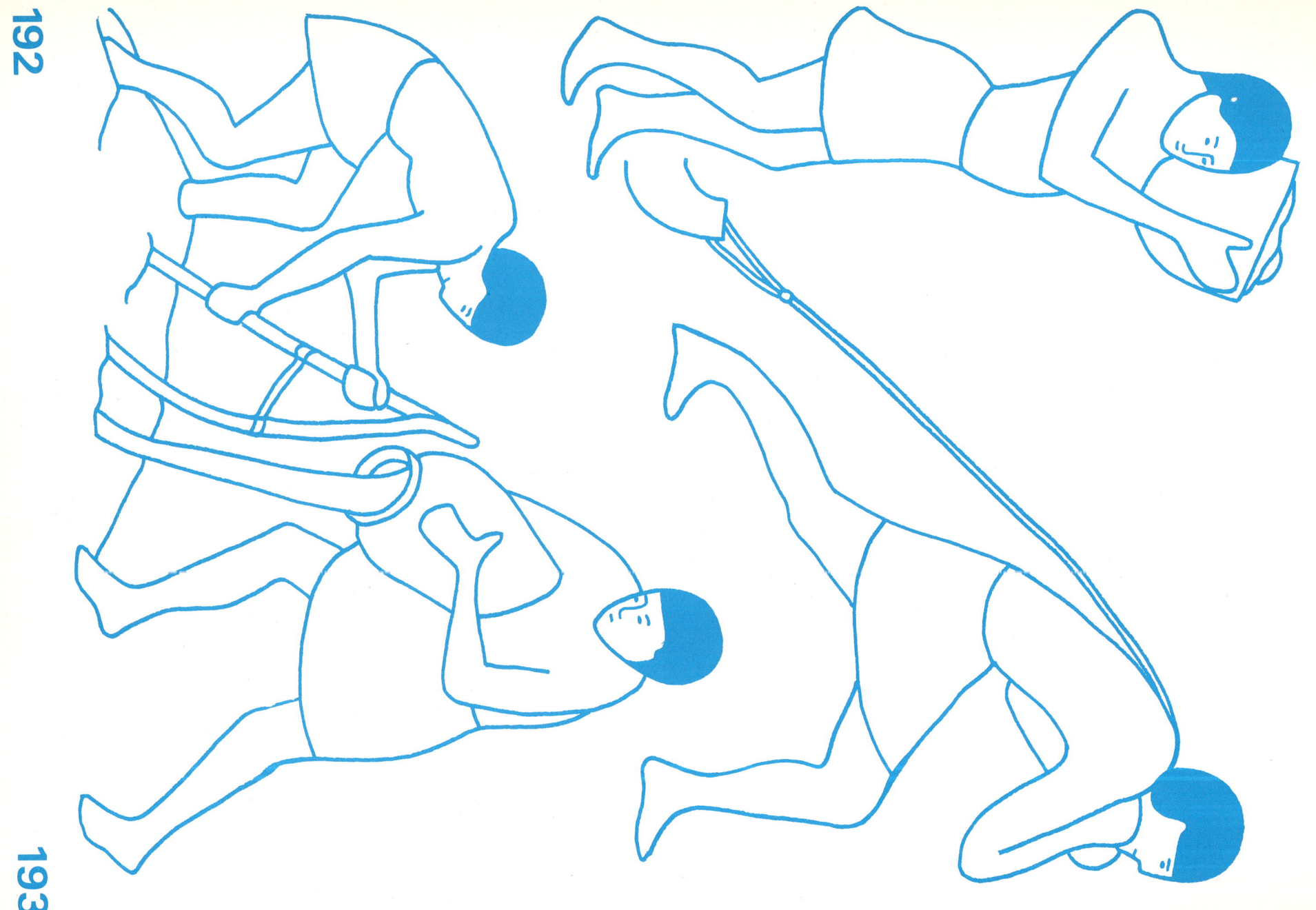

190

192

191

193

CHARACTERS

196

194

195

197

CHARACTERS

Trades and recreations

Musicians,
instruments:
198–209

Pots, potter:
210–223

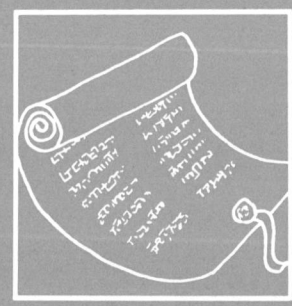
Scrolls, scribe:
224–228

Trading:
229–231

Carpentry:
232–240

Child care:
241–246

198   199   200

201   202

203

204   205

206   207 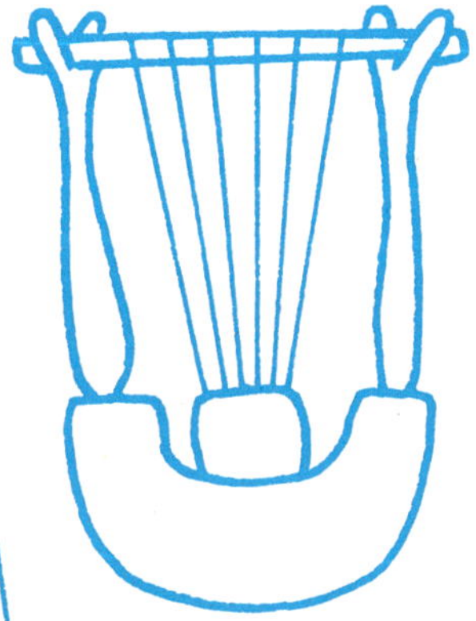   208    209

TRADES AND RECREATIONS

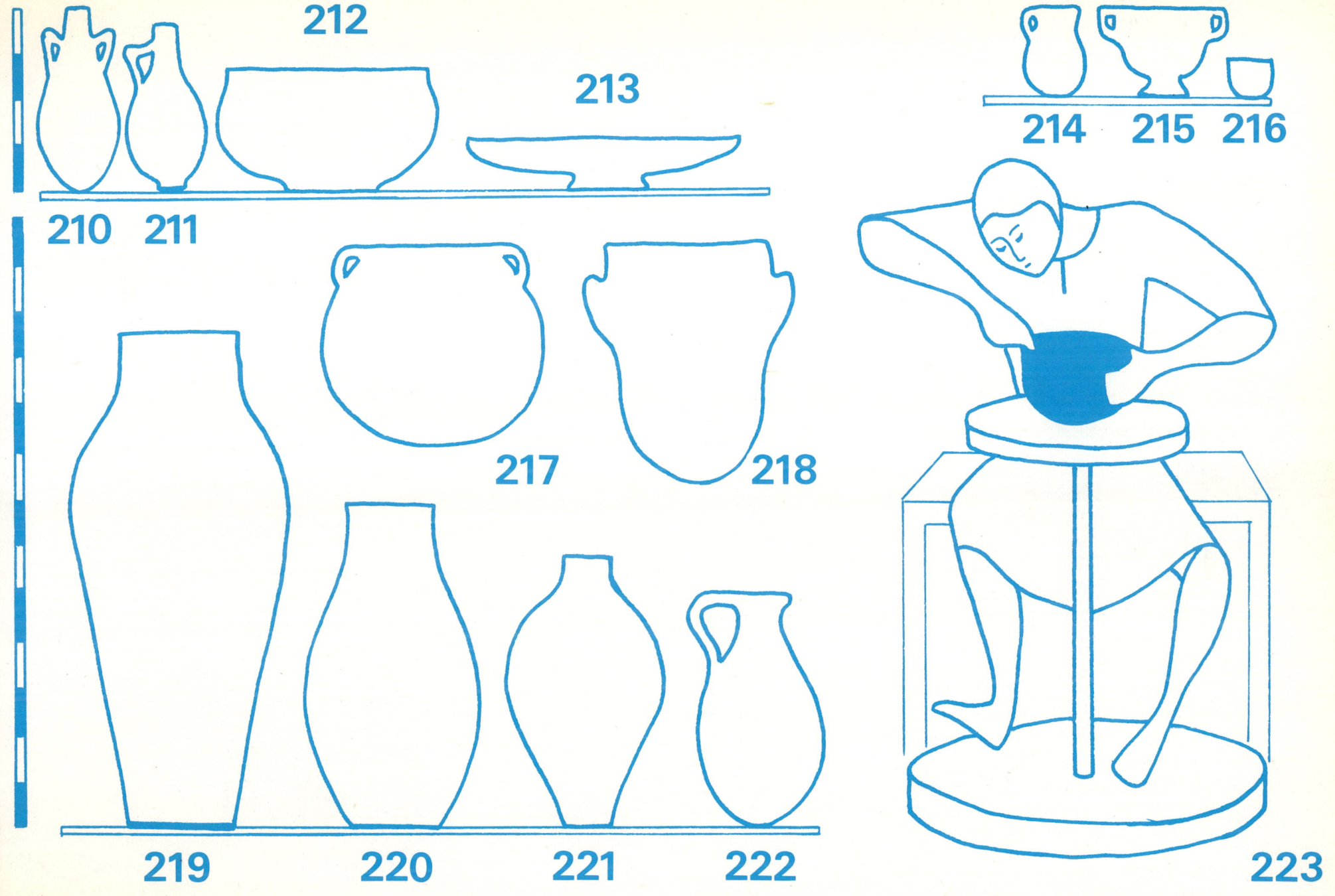

210 211 212 213 214 215 216 217 218 219 220 221 222 223

TRADES AND RECREATIONS

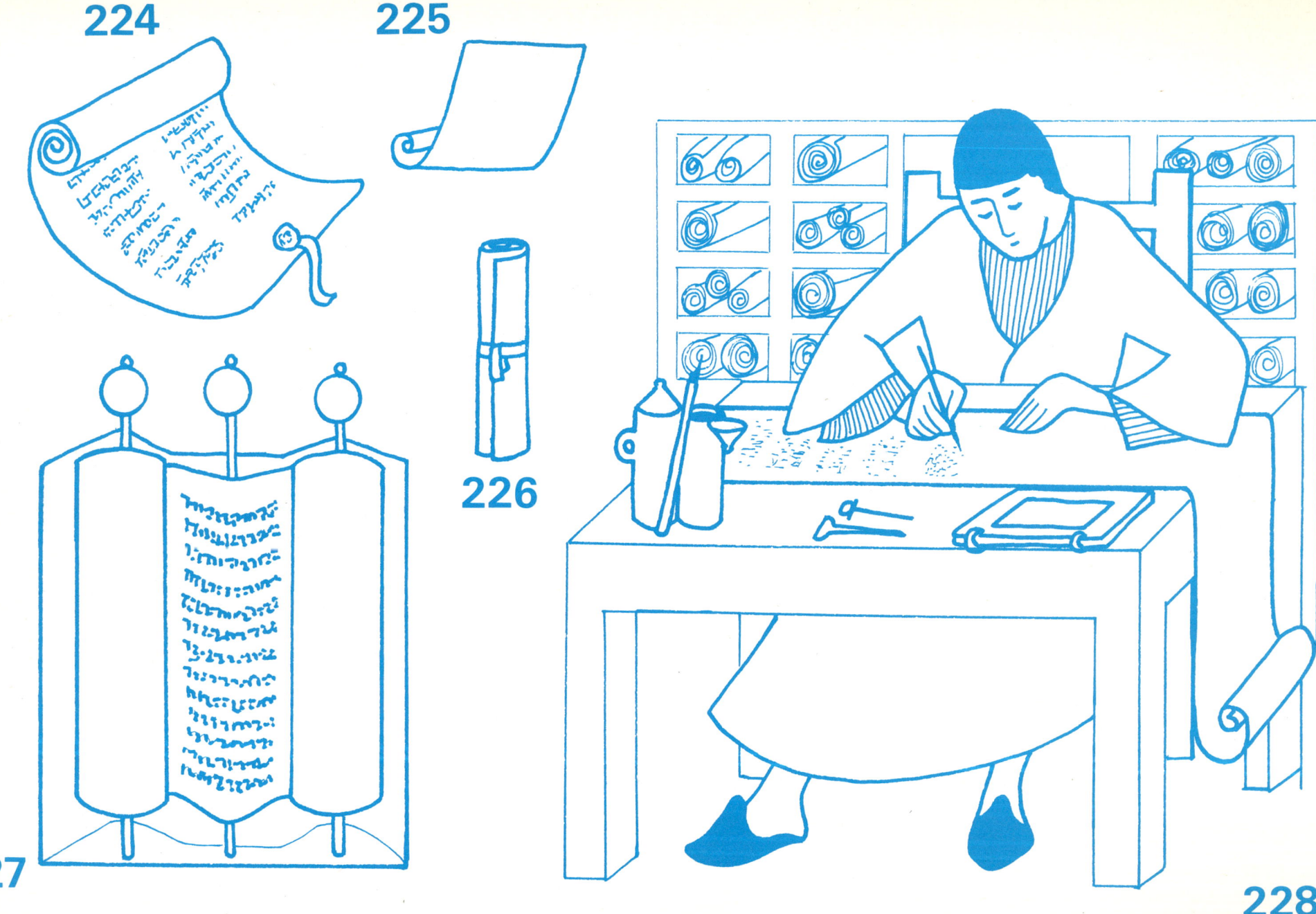

224

225

226

227

228

TRADES AND RECREATIONS

229

230

231

TRADES AND RECREATIONS

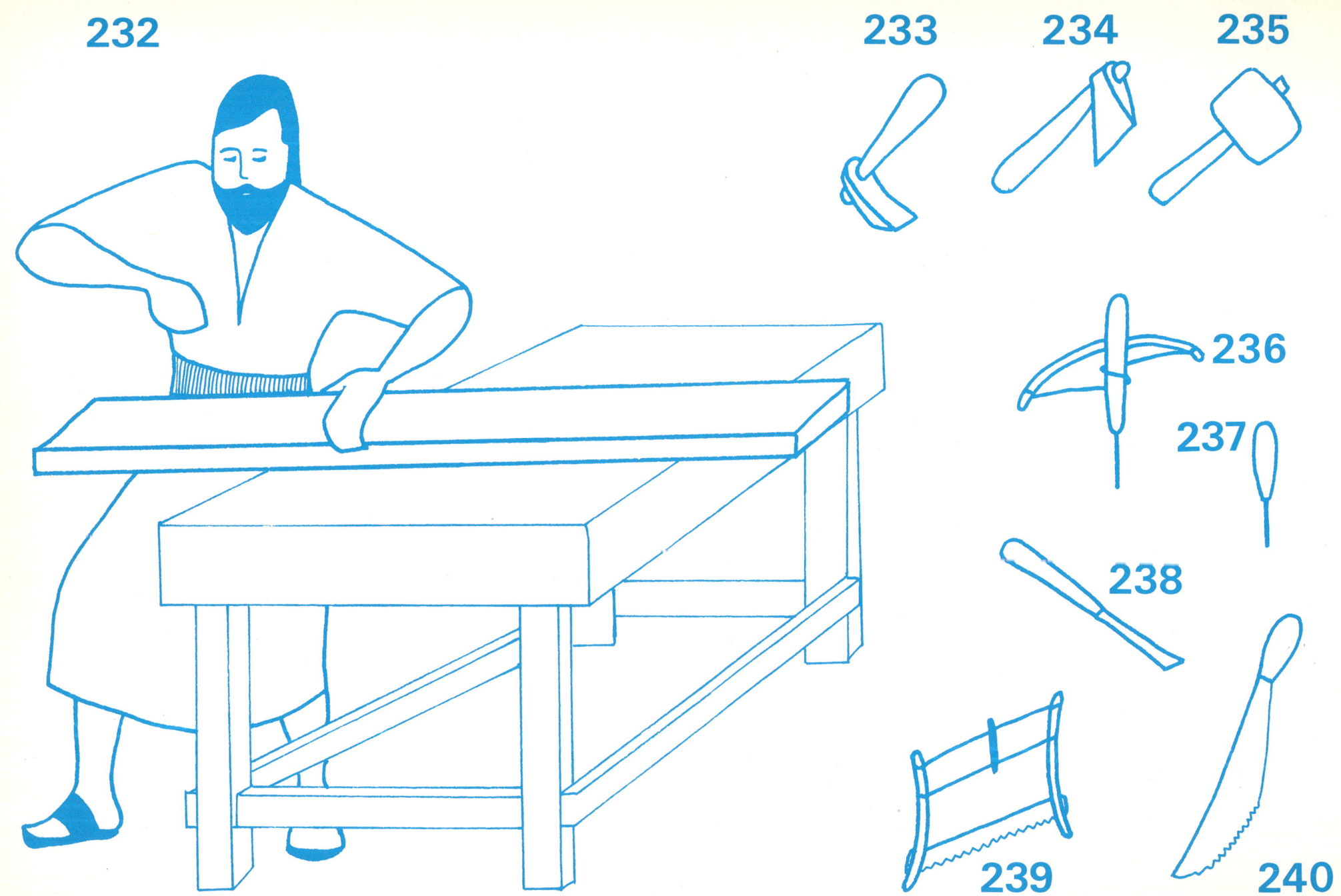

232

233 234 235

236

237

238

239 240

TRADES AND RECREATIONS

243

245

242

244

246

241

TRADES AND RECREATIONS

Occupations

Women at work:
247–255

Shepherds:
256–258

In the fields:
259–264

Baskets, carriers:
265–278

Disciples fishing:
279–284

Tax collection:
285–290

247

248

249

250

251

OCCUPATIONS

252

254

253

255

OCCUPATIONS

256   257   258

OCCUPATIONS

259

260

OCCUPATIONS

261

262

263　　264

265   266   267   268

269   270   271

OCCUPATIONS

272

273

274

275

276

277

278

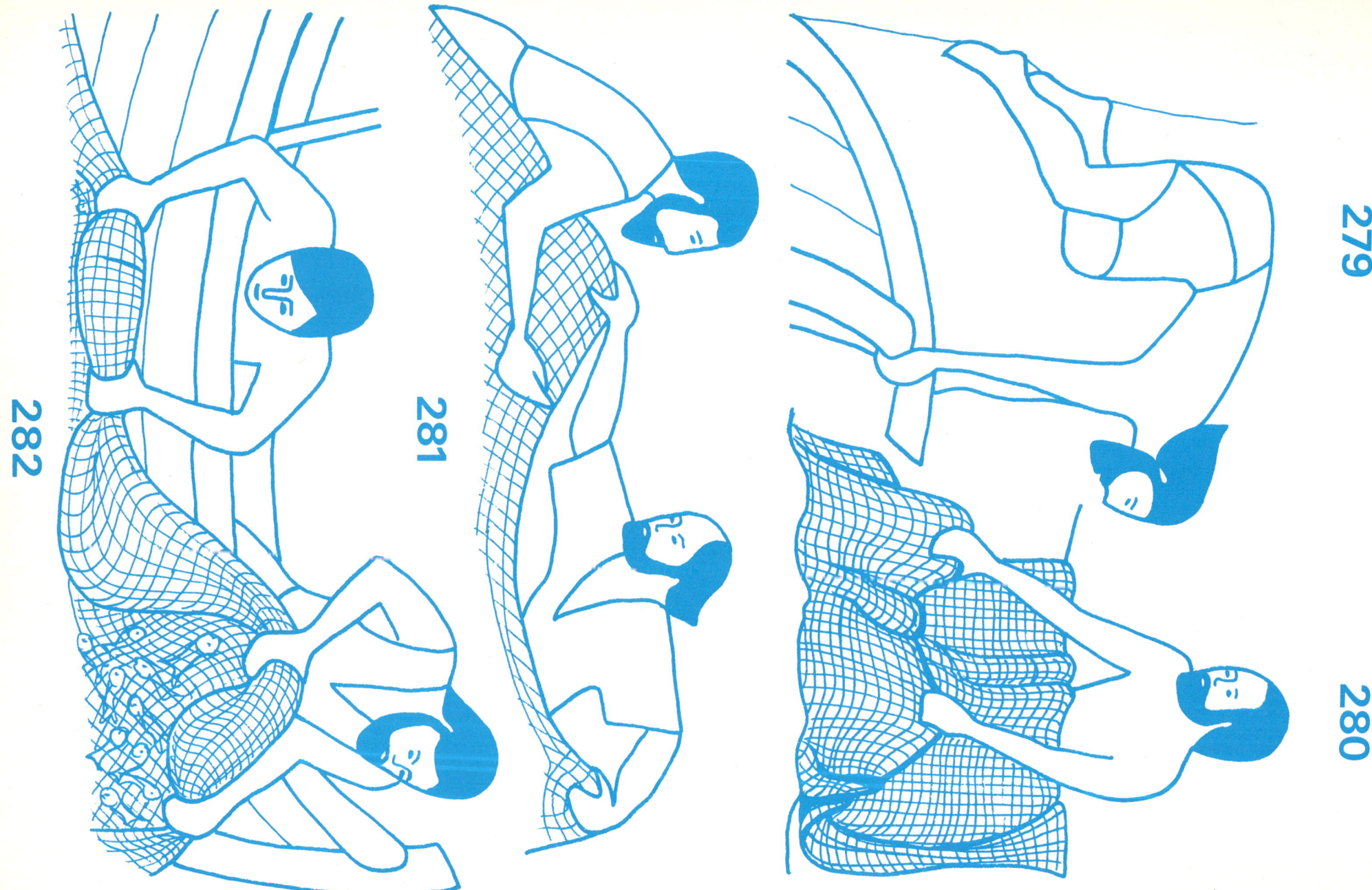

279

280

281

282

OCCUPATIONS

283

284

OCCUPATIONS

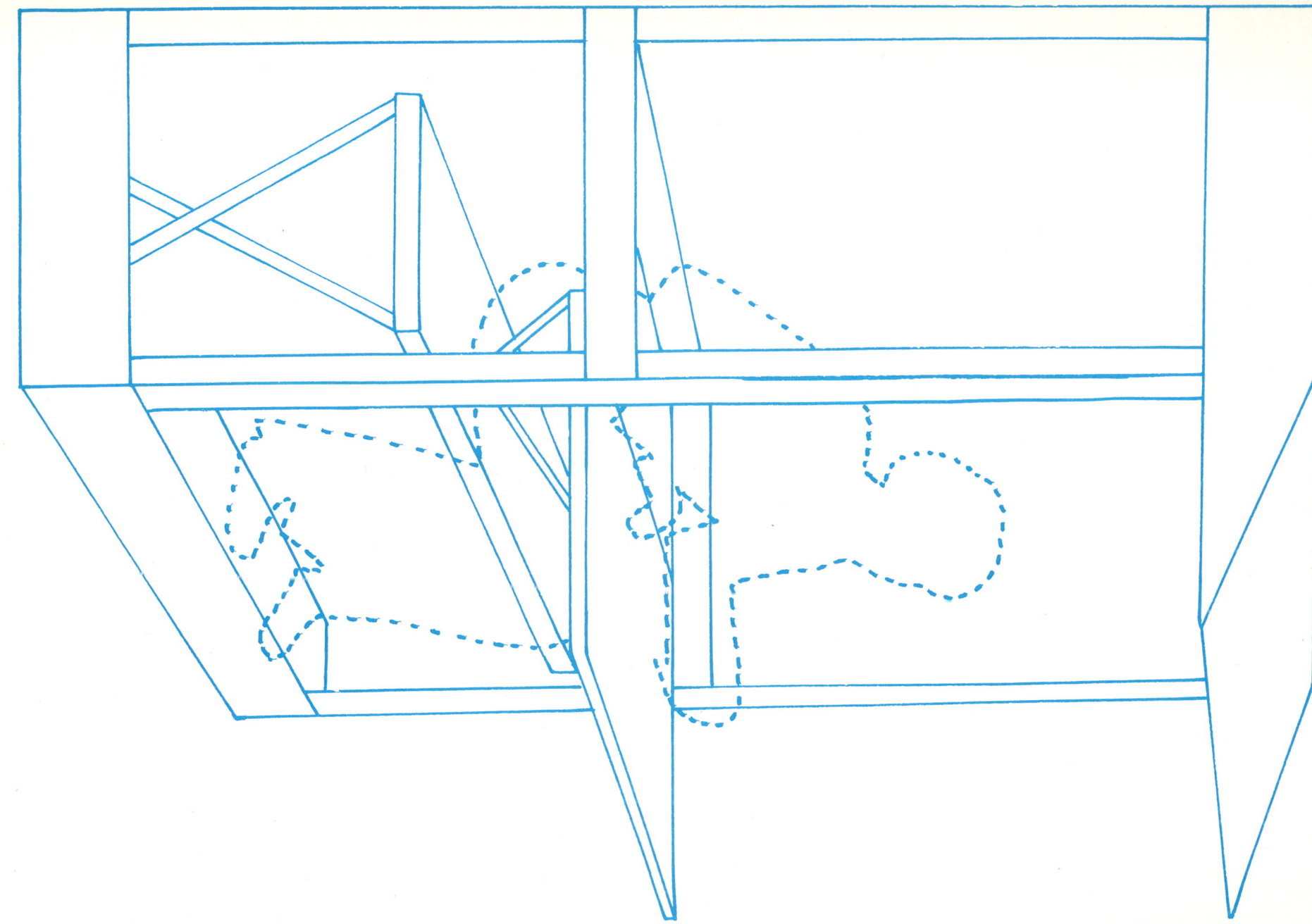

285

OCCUPATIONS

288

289

290

286

287

OCCUPATIONS

Transport

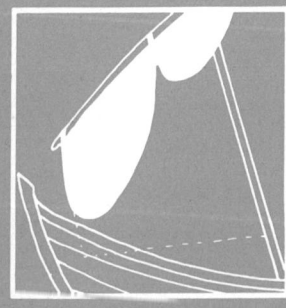

Ships, sea:
291–298

Overland:
299–301

291

292

293

TRANSPORT

TRANSPORT

TRANSPORT

TRANSPORT

298

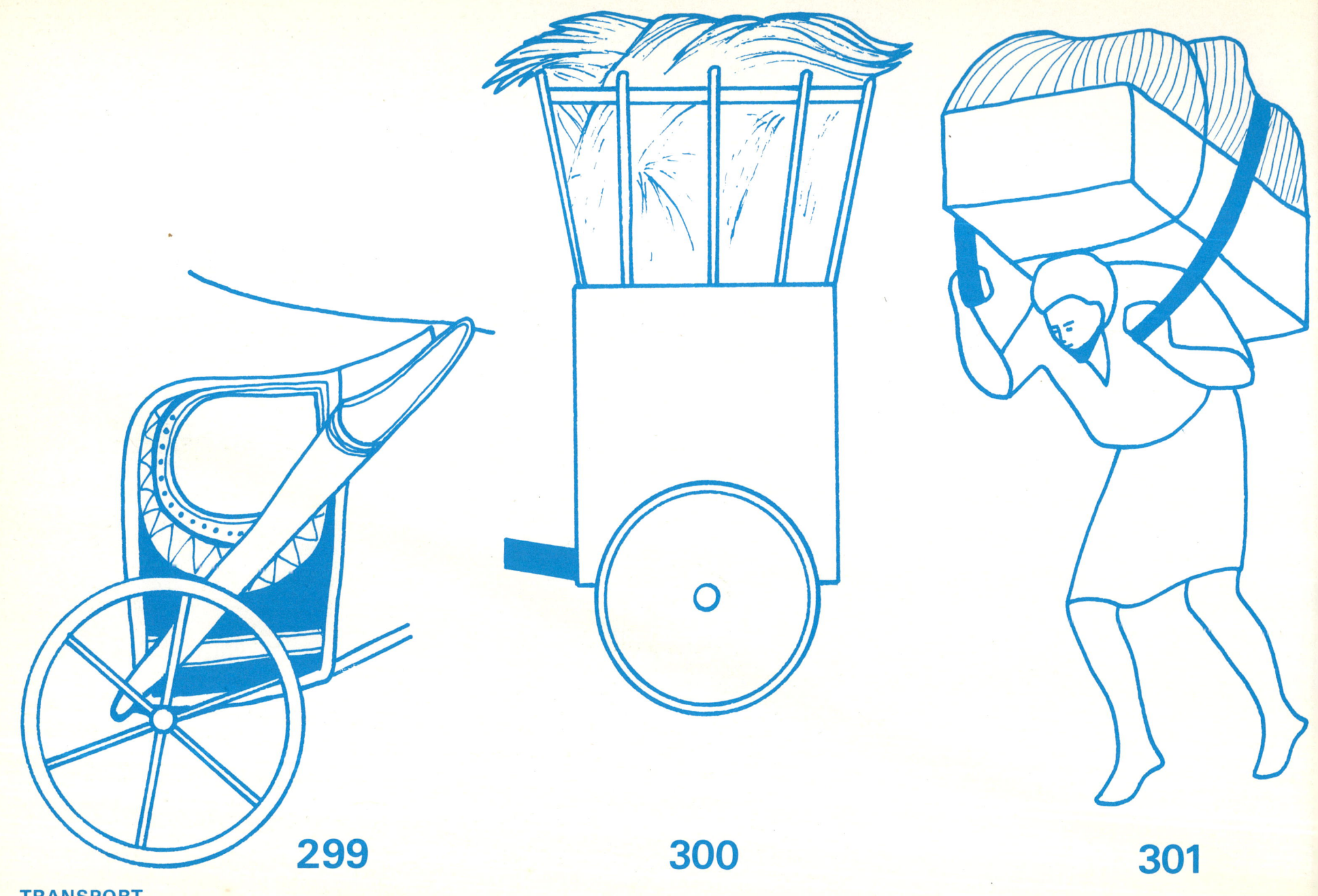

299

300

301

TRANSPORT